The Original Vegan Cookbook for Beginners

Healthy and Tasty Recipes for Every Day incl. Vegan Dessert Special

Jacob Davies

ISBN- 9798681321958

Table of Contents

What is veganism?

Contrary to popular belief, veganism isn't some new-age fad diet. Back in 1944 The Vegan Society was founded as an official offshoot of The Vegetarian Society. The two organisations differ in ethos due to vegans choosing to not only consume animal flesh, but all animal derived products.

The Vegan Society officially defines veganism as:

> *"A philosophy and way of living which seeks to exclude—as far as is possible and practicable—all forms of exploitation of, and cruelty to, animals for food, clothing or any other purpose; and by extension, promotes the development and use of animal-free alternatives for the benefit of animals, humans and the environment. In dietary terms it denotes the practice of dispensing with all products derived wholly or partly from animals."*

Therefore, veganism is not solely a diet, but in fact a life philosophy promoting equality and respect for all sentient beings. Vegans will not use leather or animal-based materials, cosmetics and products that undergo animal testing, animal by-products (eg. eggs or milk), and ethically ambiguous products- such as palm oil- that may technically be vegan, but the industry practices and consequences go against the fundamental vegan morals.

People do not necessarily adopt a vegan lifestyle when following a vegan diet however- some find the all-encompassing nature of the vegan lifestyle can be daunting and difficult to constantly adhere to. But to simply adopt a vegan diet still reaps incredible benefits, both for individual health and societal impact.

To put it simply, veganism is a lifestyle that aims to minimise personal engagement with the exploitation of animals. Individuals may adopt this lifestyle for a variety of reasons, but most commonly for personal health, ethical beliefs, and environmental activism. Veganism is an overall life philosophy, but to embrace the vegan diet one does not have to commit to all changes at once.

What foods can and can't be eaten in a vegan diet?

The vegan diet may be plant based, but this in no way limits the culinary possibilities at an imaginative vegan's fingertips!

Vegans do not eat products originating or derived from animals, such as:

- Meat (beef, lamb, pork, poultry, game, etc.)
- Fish (including shellfish)
- Eggs (including mayonnaise and albumen products)
- Dairy (animal milk, casein, cheeses, yoghurt, butter, cream, etc.)
- Gelatine or Isinglass
- Whey
- Carmine colouring
- Honey
  some vegans will still use honey as there is debate over the inclusion of insects as animals

So it's pretty simple really- if it comes from animals, it's a no-go! That means that there's so much delicious food out there to be included in a vegan diet.

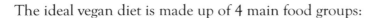

The ideal vegan diet is made up of 4 main food groups:

- ❧ Legumes, nuts, and seeds
  4+ servings a day
- ❧ Grains
  6+ servings a day
- ❧ Vegetables
  4+ servings a day
- ❧ Fruit
  2+ servings a day

This is an extremely basic breakdown of vegan nutrition, but it does demonstrate that the main nutritional elements of carbohydrates, proteins, and fats are plentiful within the vegan diet.

Some vegans find eating adequate protein a struggle when transitioning lifestyles, so we have included below a list of popular vegan protein sources:

SEITAN	25g protein / 100g
TOFU	17g protein / 100g
TEMPEH	19g protein / 100g
LENTILS	9g protein / 100g
LEGUMES	7-10g protein / 100g
SPELT	5.5g protein / 100g
QUINOA	4.4g protein / 100g
SOY MILK	4g protein / 100ml

... that's vegan?!

You may also be surprised to hear that a lot of common supermarket foods are unintentionally vegan! There's no need to throw out all your favourite snacks and blitz your whole kitchen- especially as veganism has grown in popularity a lot of brands have eagerly released vegan friendly alternative products. Check out the list below and jump with joy! All these popular foods are accidentally vegan:

- Oreos
- Ritz crackers
- Spicy Sweet Chilli Doritos
- Airheads
- Kettle brand crisps
- Skittles
- Monster Energy Drinks
- Red Bull
- Walkers Sunbites
- Lindt 70%, 85%, and 90% chocolates
- Belvita breakfast biscuits
- Nature Valley granola bars
- Sour Patch Kids
- Hershey's chocolate syrup
- Pringles original
- Starbursts

- ❧ Nairn's Biscuits
- ❧ Shreddies cereal
- ❧ McDonalds and Burger King fries
- ❧ Just Rol croissants

Who would've guessed?! So as you can see, the vegan diet may initially appear somewhat limiting, but in reality it's becoming increasingly easy to adopt veganism without having to make drastic lifestyle changes.

Health benefits of adopting a vegan lifestyle

Veganism doesn't just benefit animals or the environment- it has significant health benefits for *you* if undertaken responsibly.

It is essential to plan your vegan diet prior to transitioning. If undertaken carelessly it is extremely easy to deny yourself sufficient amounts of nutrients like B12, iron, and calcium. Dependent upon the nature of your vegan diet it may also be necessary to take supplements- discuss with your doctor beforehand to plan around your individual needs.

So what are the main health benefits veganism can offer you?

WEIGHT LOSS
Multiple studies have shown that vegans tend to have a lower BMI than the general population, and when compared against calorie-controlled diets those who went vegan lost weight more effectively. There are a variety of reasons for these findings, but most agree that the high volume of low-calorie foods decreases hunger, and overall, less calories are consumed.

LOWERED RISK OF HEART DISEASE
Increased consumption of fresh fruits, vegetables, fibre, whole grains, and nuts is extremely beneficial for cardiac health and reducing dietary factors that are often linked to heart diseases. A diet rich in these foods also aids in reducing blood sugar and cholesterol levels, further lowering the risk of heart disease.

POSSIBLE REDUCTION IN THE RISK OF CANCER
Diet plays a significant role in an individual's susceptibility to cancers. The vegetable, legume, and soya heavy nature of a vegan diet complements the

findings of a variety of studies that determined such foods played preventative roles in the development of prostate, breast, and colon cancers.

BETTER MANAGEMENT OF TYPE 2 DIABETES

Evidence suggests that vegans have lower blood sugar levels than the general population. In addition to this, their insulin sensitivity is increased, both of which may help prevent developing type 2 diabetes. For those already suffering with diabetes a vegan diet can help in the management of blood sugar levels and increase kidney function, therefore reducing the risk of further medical issues developing as a result of insulin mismanagement.

Tips and tricks for transitioning to a vegan diet

Start gradually

It's recommended to change your diet gradually- 1 vegan day a week, or one vegan meal a day- to give your body (and brain) time to adjust. It's better to transition gradually and maintain your veganism, rather than jumping straight in and creating unrealistic expectations.

Be colourful!

Try to include lots of colour on your plate. Not only does your meal look more appetizing and exciting, but a variety of colour indicates a variety of nutrients without you having to worry.

Freezer meals

Instead of throwing away any leftovers freeze them, or cook a 'safety' meal, portion it, and freeze. On those days when you can't be bothered or don't have the time to cook, you'll have a delicious homemade meal at the ready.

Try new cuisines

A lot of cultures naturally have more plant-based diets. Take your taste buds to India, Mexico, Asia and beyond- it's a great way to upgrade your cooking skills, slowly transition, and get inspiration for easy vegan dishes.

Stock up on tinned beans

Chickpeas, lentil, cannellini beans and beyond, legumes are key to the vegan diet. Stock up on tins of various beans so you'll always have something on hand to whip up a tasty and protein-packed vegan meal.

Get some #inspiration

There's loads of vegan bloggers and influencers out there, so follow them and recipe pages on social media. Not only will it provide you with inspiration and motivation, it's also a great way to connect with likeminded people and learn from their experiences.

Switch up ground meat for mushrooms and lentils

One of the easiest ways to make the average recipe vegan is to swap the meat out for a vegan alternative. Lentils and mushrooms are a great substitute for ground meat because of their texture and complementary flavour to traditionally rich and meaty sauces.

Try meat alternatives

There's lots of brands out there entirely dedicated to producing realistic meat substitutes for vegans and vegetarians. Give these a go if you're transitioning from an omnivore diet to ease yourself off meat.

Treat yourself

Vegans don't only eat kale and chickpeas! There's loads of recipes and ready made sweet treats out there, and you should treat yourself! Try some of the delicious desserts included in this book to satisfy your sweet tooth and remember the huge diversity of vegan foods you can sample.

BREAKFAST AND BRUNCH

THE ESSENTIAL VEGAN PANCAKE RECIPE

This 3-ingredient pancake recipe is a delicious and versatile way to start the day

2	SERVES
509	CALORIES
93g	CARBOHYDRATES
17.4g	PROTEIN
8.5g	FAT

INGREDIENTS

- 240g // 3c rolled oats
- 480ml // 2c nut milk
- 2 medium bananas, overripe and mashed
- Maple syrup and fresh berries to serve

DIRECTIONS

1. Place your oats into a food processor and blend until they have been broken down into flour, then add your nut milk and mashed banana, and beat until a thick batter forms

2. Heat a medium frying pan on low, ensuring the pan is hot before you add your batter. Add ¼ of your batter at a time, leaving until the bottom is browned and bubbles begin to form at the edges before flipping

3. Transfer to plates and serve with a drizzle of maple syrup and fresh berries

VARIATIONS

Cinnamon and apple
add 2tsp of cinnamon to your batter and top with stewed apple

Chocolate chip
sprinkle a few chocolate chips over the top of your pancake prior to flipping when frying

Matcha powder
add 2tsp of matcha powder to your batter

Coconut sugar and flakes
add 1tbsp of coconut sugar to your batter and top with coconut yoghurt/ cream, and a sprinkling of dried coconut chips

'SNICKERS' BREAKFAST BAR

A healthy breakfast bar version of the popular chocolate bar, make ahead of time and grab for an on-the-go breakfast or sweet snack

8	SERVES
274	CALORIES
19g	CARBOHYDRATES
10g	PROTEIN
17g	FAT

INGREDIENTS

- 120ml // 1/2c date syrup
- 80g // 1c rolled oats
- 240g // 1c peanut butter- we used smooth, but try crunchy for some extra texture
- ½ tsp salt
- 45g // ¼ c dark chocolate chips

DIRECTIONS

1. Before starting, line a square 8x8 baking tin

2. Place your peanut butter, maple syrup, salt, and oats in a small saucepan over a low heat. Stir continuously until everything has melted and formed a smooth, thick liquid, then pour the mixture over the oats and stir until thoroughly combined. Pour your mixture into your prepared tin, being sure to press it down so it is even and reaches into the corners of the tin

3. Place the baking tin in the fridge, and whilst the mixture begins to set melt your chocolate chips in the microwave- check and stir at 10 second intervals to prevent from burning until all the chocolate is melted

4. Remove your tin from the fridge and pour over the chocolate, spreading it out to form a thin layer over the entire mix. Return to the fridge to set for a minimum of 30 minutes. Once set, remove from the fridge and cut into 8 bars. Store them in the fridge to keep the fudgy texture and chocolate crunch

AVOCADO TOAST

Not just for hipsters, avocado on toast has endless variations! We've included the bare essentials here and some inspiration, but let yourself go wild with toppings, mashing techniques, and spices

1	SERVES
237	CALORIES
21.4g	CARBOHYDRATES
6.1g	PROTEIN
15.8g	FAT

INGREDIENTS

- 1 slice of bread - we recommend rye, wholegrain, or sourdough
- ½ a ripe avocado

DIRECTIONS

1. Place your bread in the toaster and set so it is crispy, but still soft within

2. In a bowl mash your avocado to your preference- we like it 'smashed' aka uneven mashing to create some texture

3. Once brown and crispy, smear the avocado onto your toast. Enjoy as it is, or try one of the variations suggested below

VARIATIONS

Top your avocado with chopped tomato and fresh basil, and drizzle over a balsamic glaze

Add chilli flakes and 1 tbsp of lemon juice when mashing your avocado

Top your avocado with chickpeas before adding a generous drizzle of siracha sauce

Toss together chopped strawberries and pineapple to create a fruit salsa topping

Sautee mushrooms, onion, and fresh garlic to serve atop or on the side of your toast

FRENCH TOAST

The soaked chia seeds work as a substitute for the egg found in your classic French toast. Soft bread, lightly fried and sweet- you can never go wrong with French toast

5	SERVES
165	CALORIES
37g	CARBOHYDRATES
8g	PROTEIN
4g	FAT

INGREDIENTS

- ½ tsp ground cinnamon
- ½ tsp vanilla extract
- Pinch of salt
- 240 ml // 1c nut milk
- 1 tbsp chia seeds
- ½ tbsp maple syrup
- 5 slices of thick sliced bread
- 1 tbsp coconut oil for frying

DIRECTIONS

1. In a large, shallow bowl mix the seeds, syrup, milk, and flavourings. Place this mixture into the fridge for 15 minutes

2. After 15 minutes melt your coconut oil in a frying pan on a medium heat. Whilst this heats up remove your chia mix from the fridge and dip each slice of bread in the mix- be sure to thoroughly soak each side. Place the soaked bread into the pan, and fry each side for 3-4 minutes, or until crisped and golden brown

3. Remove from the pan and serve as desired- try topping with fresh fruit and coconut cream, or nut butter and sliced banana

FRUITY QUINOA PORRIDGE

An upgrade on the average porridge, we've included a fruity quinoa version but feel free to experiment with different milks, toppings, and oat:quinoa ratios

2	SERVES
271	CALORIES
39g	CARBOHYDRATES
8g	PROTEIN
4g	FAT

INGREDIENTS

- 2tbsp dried cranberries
- 3 strips of dried mango, sliced
- 50g // 1/2 c rolled oats
- 50g // 1/4c quinoa
- 120ml // ½ c orange juice
- 120ml // 1/2c water
- 250ml // 1c nut milk
- 2 peaches, cut into slices
- 1tsp maple syrup

DIRECTIONS

1. The night before cooking place your dried cranberries and orange juice into a bowl. Leave to soak, and in the morning separate the juice from the rehydrated berries

2. Place the dried mango, quinoa, oats, juice, and water into a small saucepan. Gently heat until simmering, and once simmering leave for 15 minutes to thicken, being sure to stir occasionally. Once thickened pour in the nut milk and leave on the heat for a further 5 minutes

3. When the porridge reaches your desired consistency remove it from the heat and serve, topping with the sliced peaches, rehydrated cranberries, and a drizzle of maple syrup. Serve immediately

MANGO AND COCONUT SMOOTHIE BOWL

Cool and creamy, this tropical smoothie bowl is a healthy way to get up and going!

1	SERVES
414	CALORIES
44g	CARBOHYDRATES
8g	PROTEIN
22g	FAT

INGREDIENTS

- 1 banana, frozen
- 120g // 2/3 c mango, frozen
- 60ml // ¼ c mango juice
- 100ml // 1/3 c+1tbsp coconut milk
- 4tbsp coconut milk yoghurt
- Coconut flakes, granola, mango slices, and granadilla to serve

DIRECTIONS

1. Place your frozen fruit, mango juice, coconut milk, and coconut yoghurt in a food processor. Blend on high until all the fruit is blended and a thick, creamy consistency forms

2. Spoon into a bowl and serve with extra mango slices, your favourite granola, granadilla pulp, and a sprinkling of coconut flakes

FRIED EGG..?!

If you're craving a fry-up try this fried egg alternative. It's high in protein and great for topping potato cakes or toast

4	SERVES
182	CALORIES
4g	CARBOHYDRATES
10g	PROTEIN
4g	FAT

INGREDIENTS

Yolk

- 2tbsp vegetable oil
- 2tsp nutritional yeast
- ¼ tsp turmeric
- 1/8 tsp mustard powder
- ½ tsp kala namak
- 240ml // 1c water
- 4tsp cornflour

White

- 1 block of tofu, approximately 200-350g
- 1tbsp coconut oil
- Salt and pepper to taste

DIRECTIONS

1. To start, make your 'yolk'. Do this by whisking your water and cornflour together in a small saucepan until the cornflour has dissolved. Add your remaining 'yolk' ingredients, and transfer to the stove

2. Cook the mixture over a high heat, whisking continuously. The sauce will thicken, and you will know it is ready once it coats the back of a wooden spoon- between 3-5 minutes of cooking

3. Whilst the sauce cools, prepare your 'white' by cutting your tofu into thin slices (4 or 8 depending the size of your block), and trimming each slice to create a circle. Heat your oil in a frying pan, and once melted add the 'whites', one at a time. Cook for 2-4 minutes each side, or until browned and crispy at the edges

4. Serve by cutting a hole in the fried 'white' and adding a spoonful of the 'yolk' sauce. Season with salt and pepper to taste

CINNAMON ROLLS

Have them for breakfast, brunch, or a sweet treat! These cinnamon rolls are guaranteed to leave you smiling with their light dough and classic filling

10	SERVES
249	CALORIES
35g	CARBOHYDRATES
4.7g	PROTEIN
9g	FAT

INGREDIENTS

Dough

- 3tbsp vegan butter
- 240ml // 1c almond milk, unsweetened
- 1tbsp brown sugar

- 1 packet instant yeast (7g)
- ½ tsp salt
- 400g // 3c plain flour

Filling

- 4tbsp vegan butter, melted
- 50g // ¼ c brown sugar
- 4tsp ground cinnamon
- 1tsp ground nutmeg
- 2tbsp vegan butter to top

DIRECTIONS

1. To start, make your dough. Do this by first heating your 3tbsp vegan butter and almond milk in a saucepan, over a low heat to prevent it from boiling. Remove from the heat and allow to cool slightly

2. Once warm, but not hot, pour the liquid into a large mixing bowl and sprinkle over the yeast with 1tbsp of sugar and leave for 10 minutes, or until the mixture becomes frothy

3. When the mix has activated add your salt and flour. Instead adding all your flour at once add a couple of tbsp at a time, mix, and add more. When the mixture is sticky and you can no longer stir it (you may not need all the flour) transfer it to a floured surface and knead the dough for a couple of minutesWhen it can easily form a ball and isn't too sticky transfer the dough to a lightly oiled bowl and cover with a clean dishcloth or clingfilm. Leave to prove in a warm place until doubled in size- at least 1 hour. Whilst the dough proves make your filling by mixing your brown sugar, nutmeg, and cinnamon into the melted butter until it forms a paste

4. When the dough has proved roll it out onto a floured surface so it forms a rectangle, and is roughly 1cm in thickness. Using a knife or brush spread on your cinnamon paste, evenly covering all the dough

5. Cut your dough into 10 evenly sized strips. Roll the strips up and place them into an oiled 8x baking tin. Melt your remaining 2tbsp of vegan butter and brush it over the rolls, before covering once again and leaving to prove for a further 30 minutes. Preheat your oven to 180C/350F as they prove

6. Bake your rolls for 25-30mins, or until golden brown. Remove from the oven and serve immediately

■□■□■□■□■□■□■□

EASIEST EVER BREAKFAST SANDWICH

Like a sausage bap, but better! This sandwich is a cross between a sausage or bacon butty and eggs benedict, but definitely the fancy version

1	SERVES
573	CALORIES
44g	CARBOHYDRATES
21g	PROTEIN
35g	FAT

INGREDIENTS

- 1 vegan sausage patty
- Handful of spinach
- 3 button mushrooms, sliced or diced
- 1tbsp Vegan mayo
- ½ tsp smoked paprika
- 1 English muffin
- ¼ avocado sliced
- 1tsp coconut oil for frying

DIRECTIONS

1. Melt your coconut oil in a frying pan on a high heat. Add your patty and fry for a couple of minutes on either side so it is browned and crispy, then transfer to a plate and set aside

2. Keep the frying pan on the stove and add your sliced mushrooms. Once they begin to colour add your spinach and fry for a further couple of minutes to wilt your spinach. Turn off the heat and set aside

3. Cut your muffin in half and toast. As it toasts mix together your mayo and paprika, and slice your avocado. To serve, take your muffin and spread the smoked mayo on one half. Layer with the sautéed mushrooms and spinach, before adding your patty. Top with your sliced avocado and the rest of the muffin. Eat whilst still warm

TOFU SCRAMBLE

Once again using tofu as an egg substitute, you'll barely realise it's not the real deal! Creamy and flavoursome, you can have this for breakfast, lunch, and dinner

2	SERVES
206	CALORIES
3.8g	CARBOHYDRATES
20.3g	PROTEIN
13.1g	FAT

INGREDIENTS

- 220g // 1c tofu, firm
- 1tbsp vegan butter
- 2tbsp nutritional yeast
- ½ tsp turmeric
- ½ tsp ground cumin
- ½ tsp garlic powder
- ¼ tsp onion powder
- 60ml // 1/4 c soy milk

DIRECTIONS

1. Place your tofu in a medium bowl and mash unevenly with a fork- leave some chunks for texture, but nothing too big. Add your seasonings to the bowl and mix gently, being careful to not break your tofu up and further. Once combined pour in the soya milk, and once again mix gently

2. In a medium pan melt your butter. Once melted spoon the tofu, leaving most of the liquid in the bowl. Fry the tofu until lightly browned, then slowly pour in the remaining liquid whilst stirring. The tofu will absorb the liquid, so keep on the heat until your desired consistency is reached

3. Transfer to a plate and serve. We suggest serving it on toast, topped with fried tomatoes and avocado

LUNCHES AND DINNERS

RUBY TART TATIN

Sweet beetroot and apple with tart balsamic- this savoury tart tatin is a lovely addition to any vegan get together

6	SERVES
444	CALORIES
40g	CARBOHYDRATES
6g	PROTEIN
27g	FAT

INGREDIENTS

- 1 block of vegan puff pastry (and a sprinkling of flour to roll)
- 400g // 2 ½ c beetroot, cut into bite sized chunks
- 1 small apple, peeled and cut into bite sized chunks
- 1 large red onion, sliced
- 2tbsp brown sugar
- 2tbsp rice wine vinegar
- 3tbsp olive oil
- Balsamic vinegar and leafy greens to serve

DIRECTIONS

1. Before starting, preheat your oven to 180C/350F, and oil a large ovenproof frying pan, or a circular baking tin

2. Place your beetroot, apple, sliced red onion, sugar, vinegar, salt and pepper to season, and oil in a large bowl. Using a spoon or your hands mix everything together, ensuring that all the veg is coated in oil and vinegar. Pour the mix into your oiled tin, cover with foil, and bake in the preheated oven for 45 minutes

3. On a floured surface roll out your pastry so it is 0.5cm thick. Cut out a circle slightly wider than tin- add 1-1.5cm extra to the edge. Remove your veg from the oven. Take a dishcloth and press down on the tinfoil to pack your veg together, before removing the tinfoil entirely. Place your rolled dough over the tin, and using a knife or spoon press the pastry border into the tin, effectively creating a dome over your veg

4. Return to the oven and cook for a further 30-40 minutes, or until the top is puffed, golden, and crispy. Remove from the oven and loosen the edges with a knife, before turning onto a large plate

5. Cut into slices and serve drizzled with balsamic vinegar and accompanied by a leafy greens salad on the side

THAI GREEN CURRY

Potato, tofu, and beans make this thai green curry as filling as it is tasty, with the coconut milk ensuring a beautifully creamy sauce base

4	SERVES
436	CALORIES
57g	CARBOHYDRATES
13g	PROTEIN
17g	FAT

INGREDIENTS

- 200g // 1c small potatoes, quartered
- 100g // 2/3 c green beans, trimmed
- 90g // ½ c broccoli florets
- 1tbsp coconut oil
- 1 garlic clove, minced
- 4tsp thai green curry paste
- 420ml // 1 ¾ c coconut milk
- 1 lime
- 80g // ½ c mangetout
- 100g // ½ c firm tofu, cut into bitesized cubes

DIRECTIONS

1. Fill a large saucepan with salted water and bring to the boil. Add your potatoes and cook for 5 minutes, before adding your green beans and broccoli and cooking for a further 3-4 minutes- you want them cooked, but still with some bite. Remove from the heat, drain, and set aside

2. Melt your oil in a medium pan over a high heat. Add your garlic and tofu, and fry until it starts to brown, then add your curry paste. Fry for another minute so the curry paste has darkened slightly and the tofu is coated and crisp, then stir in your coconut milk. Bring to a simmer, add the zest of your lime, and leave for 5 minutes to thicken

3. Once the sauce has thickened slightly add in your cooked potatoes, beans, and mangetout. Squeeze in the juice of your lime, stir to combine it all, and then remove from the heat

4. Serve immediately, either accompanied by coriander rice or as it is

BASIC BUDDAH BOWL

Fantastic for a quick and delicious meal, grab from your fridge and assemble within minutes

4	SERVES
597	CALORIES
68.8g	CARBOHYDRATES
14.4g	PROTEIN
35.2g	FAT

INGREDIENTS

- 200g // 1c short grain or brown rice
- 150g // 1c edamame beans, frozen or fresh
- 160g // 1c mangetout

Topping

- ½ cucumber, diced
- 1 carrot, peeled into ribbons
- 1 spring onion, finely sliced
- 1 lime, quartered
- 2tbsp sesame seeds
- 2 avocados, sliced

- 175g // 1c broccoli florets
- 2tbsp soy sauce
- 2 romaine lettuce heads, chopped (alternatively you can use spinach, kale, or cabbage)

DIRECTIONS

1. Bring a saucepan of salted water to the boil. Add in your rice and cook per packet instructions. Drain the rice before stirring in your soy sauce, then set aside

2. In a separate pan bring water to the boil. Add in your edamame beans and cook for 2-3 minutes, before adding your mangetout and broccoli, and cooking for a further 2 minutes. Once cooked, drain and set aside

3. Prepare your toppings before assembling your bowl. Divide your rice between 4 bowls, then layer with lettuce and your cooked, cooled veg. Sprinkle over diced cucumber, carrot ribbons, sliced green onion, and sesame seeds, before arranging your sliced avocado. Finish with a squeeze of lime

VEGETABLE PAKORAS WITH CORIANDER DIPPING SAUCE

Try for a light main or an appetizer, these pakoras are wonderfully crispy and flavoursome with every bite

4	SERVES
278	CALORIES
34.5g	CARBOHYDRATES
9.2g	PROTEIN
12g	FAT

INGREDIENTS

- 170g // ¾ c sweet potato, thinly sliced
- 1 white onion, sliced
- 1 handful of spinach, torn
- 80g // 1c fresh coriander, finely chopped
- 1 red chilli, finely sliced
- 170g // 1 1/3 c chickpea flour
- 2tsp lemon juice
- 175ml // 1/3 c water
- 1 tsp ground turmeric
- 1tsp ground cumin

- 1tsp ground coriander seeds
- 2tsp coconut oil
- 1.5l vegetable oil for deep frying

■□■□■□■□■□■□■□■□■□■□

Coriander Dipping Sauce

- 80g // 1c fresh coriander, finely chopped
- 1 handful of spinach
- 2tbsp nutritional yeast
- 60ml // ¼ c water
- 4tsp olive oil
- Salt to taste

DIRECTIONS

1. Place your flour, lemon juice, water, and spices in a medium mixing bowl and whisk together until it forms a smooth batter. When the batter is formed gently fold in your potato, onion, spinach, coriander, and finely sliced chilli

2. Heat your oil in a deep fryer or a deep, heavy bottomed saucepan. Once your oil has heated to 180C/350F start adding your pakora batter, 1 large tbsp at a time. Cook for 1-3 minutes per side, or until golden and crispy. Remove the cooked pakoras from the fryer and on a plate lined with a paper towel

3. To make your coriander dipping sauce simply place all ingredients in a food processor and blend on high. If the consistency is too thick add in extra water, 1tsp at a time, until your desired thickness is reached

4. Serve your pakoras warm with the coriander sauce and fruit chutney

CAULIFLOWER DAHL

A slight twist on the classic lentil dahl, the addition of cauliflower adds extra texture and flavour to upgrade this essential meal

4	SERVES
465	CALORIES
55.3g	CARBOHYDRATES
24.8g	PROTEIN
17.7g	FAT

INGREDIENTS

- 1 white onion, diced
- 1 clove of garlic, minced
- 1 medium cauliflower head, cut into florets
- 2tsp olive oil
- 1tbsp ground cumin
- 1tbsp ground turmeric
- 1tbsp garam masala
- 1tsp chilli flakes
- 300g // 1 ½ c yellow split peas
- 800ml // 3 1/3 c coconut milk (2 tins)
- 240ml // 1c water

DIRECTIONS

1. Heat olive oil in a large, heavy bottomed saucepan. Sautee your diced onion and minced garlic, cooking for 2-3 minutes or until softened and fragrant. Add in your spices and cook for a further 3 minutes, before pouring in the cauliflower, coconut milk, and water

2. Slowly bring the mixture to the boil, before leaving to simmer for 45minutes-1 hour. Check on the mixture every 10-15 minutes, stirring to ensure the bottom doesn't burn. If the mixture thickens too much add in water, 1tbsp at a time

3. Once the dahl has reached your desired consistency remove it from the heat. Serve warm or cold, accompanied by naan bread and topped with crispy fried onion

HERBY FALAFELS

We used fresh and dried herbs for these falafels, but the chickpea base is hugely versatile so you can experiment with different spices and additions

4	SERVES
354	CALORIES
34.6g	CARBOHYDRATES
10.9g	PROTEIN
20.7g	FAT

INGREDIENTS

- 1tbsp olive oil
- 200g // 1c chickpeas
- ½ small red onion, diced
- 15g // ½ c fresh parsley, chopped
- 15g // ½ c fresh coriander, chopped
- 4 garlic cloves, minced
- 2tsp mixed herbs
- 2tsp ground cumin
- Salt and pepper to taste

DIRECTIONS

1. Before starting, preheat your oven to 180C/350F, and oil a large baking tray

2. Place the chickpeas, onion, herbs, and garlic into a food processor and blend until smooth. As it blends mix together your turmeric and cumin, spreading it out flat on a small plate

3. Once blended make your falafel. This recipe makes 12 falafels, so scoop roughly 2tbsp for one falafel. Shape into a ball and roll in the mixed spices to cover, then transfer to your oiled baking tray

4. Bake in the centre of your oven for 20-30 minutes, being sure to flip halfway. When both sides are crispy and golden remove the tray from the oven. Serve warm from the oven, or refrigerate for a quick snack

BEAN SOUP

You can whip this bean soup up in no time for a quick, warm, filling meal. We used mixed beans, but try kidney or black beans for something new

2	SERVES
163	CALORIES
32g	CARBOHYDRATES
9g	PROTEIN
0g	FAT

INGREDIENTS

- 1 can of mixed beans
- 2 large tomatoes, diced
- 1/2 red pepper, diced
- 1tsp olive oil
- 1/2 small white onion, diced
- 1 clove of garlic, minced
- 2 tsp smoked paprika
- ½ tsp cayenne pepper
- Salt and pepper to taste
- Chopped coriander and coconut cream to serve

DIRECTIONS

1. Transfer ½ your can of beans, diced tomatoes, and red pepper to a food processor and blend until smooth, then set aside

2. In a medium, heavy bottomed pan, heat your oil before adding the onion, garlic, and spices. Sautee until soft and browned before pouring in the blended liquid. Cook the soup on a medium heat, adding water or nut milk if it appears too thick. Add the remainder of your beans and simmer on a low heat for 10-15 minutes

3. Serve immediately, topping with chopped coriander and a dollop of coconut cream if desired

MUSHROOM AND QUINOA PATTIES

These burger patties are so delicious even the most dedicated meat eater will want another! Served with a rosemary mayo, everyone will be begging you for this recipe!

4	SERVES
495	CALORIES
49g	CARBOHYDRATES
9g	PROTEIN
31g	FAT

INGREDIENTS

- 1/2 red onion, diced
- ½ white onion, diced
- 4 portobello mushrooms, washed and chopped
- 30g // 1/4c walnuts, crushed
- 2 cloves of garlic, minced

- 2tbsp olive oil
- 2tsp rice wine vinegar
- 180g // 1c quinoa, cooked per packet instructions
- 2tbsp cornflour

Mayo

- 120g // 1/2c vegan mayo
- 1tsp fresh rosemary, finely chopped

- 1tsp lemon juice
- Salt and pepper to taste

Serving

- 4 burger buns
- Lettuce

- Sliced tomatoes

DIRECTIONS

1. Before starting, preheat your oven to 200C/400F, and lightly oil a large baking tray. Add your mushrooms, walnuts, garlic, white onion, and 1 tbsp oil to the tray and toss, ensuring all the mushrooms are oiled. Bake in the centre of the oven for 20 minutes, or until tender

2. Transfer the cooked mushroom mix to a food processor and add your red onion and wine vinegar. Pulse until it is mostly blended, but still has some texture. Pour into a bowl with your cornflour and quinoa, and mix together until fully combined

3. Divide your mixture into quarters and shape into patties Place the patties back onto your baking tray, having oiled the tray once again. Cook for 10 minutes, then reduce the oven temperature to 180C/350F and cook for a further 10-15 minutes, turning halfway. The patties will be done when browned and crispy

4. Whilst the patties bake make your flavoured mayo- do this by combining all the 'mayo' ingredients and mixing thoroughly

5. When the patties are cooked remove them from the oven to cool slightly and prepare to serve. Assemble into a burger by spreading a layer of mayo onto the bottom of your bun, then topping with lettuce leaves, sliced tomatoes, and your patty. Place a skwere through the bun to hold everything in place, then serve whilst still warm

LENTIL AND COUSCOUS SALAD

A simple summer salad, the addition of juicy raisins and fresh herbs add extra depth, texture, and flavour to this picnic staple

6	SERVES
574	CALORIES
51.1g	CARBOHYDRATES
13.2g	PROTEIN
35.9g	FAT

INGREDIENTS

- 150g // ¾ c lentils (we used yellow, but green or red also work nicely)
- 150g // 1c couscous
- 3tbsp raisins
- 2 lemons, juice and zest
- 2 garlic cloves, minced
- 2 bay leaves, fresh or dried
- 1 small red onion, sliced
- 4 spring onions, the white finely sliced
- 2 large tomatoes, diced
- 2 red bell peppers, diced
- 50g // 2c fresh mint sprigs, finely chopped
- 50g // 2c fresh dill sprigs, finely chopped
- 120ml // ½ c olive oil
- Salt and pepper to taste

■□■□■□■□■□■□■□

DIRECTIONS

1. Place the couscous, raisins, lemon juice and zest in a large bowl and pour in boiling water as per packet instructions. Cover with a plate and set aside to soak and expand, stirring with a fork after 20 minutes to ensure a light texture

2. Whilst the couscous soaks bring a medium saucepan of salted water to the boil. Add your lentils, garlic, and bay leaves, and leave to simmer on a low heat for 15 minutes, or until tender but not mushy. Drain the cooked lentils and remove the bay leaves before setting aside to cool

3. In this time slice and prepare your remaining ingredients but leave a sprig of mint and dill for garnishing. Toss everything together in a large bowl, being sure to coat everything in oil and lemon juice

4. Once your couscous is soaked and your lentils have had time to cool mix the two together. Add in your vegetable mix, and thoroughly combine everything. Leave the salad in the fridge for 20-30 minutes to give the couscous and lentils time to soak up the flavours

5. Transfer to a bowl and serve, garnishing with the fresh mint and dill

CURRIED CARROT PITTAS

Glowing orange, these pittas are as tasty as they are attractive. The curried carrot is reminiscent of corination chicken, especially with the addition of raisins or peanuts

4	SERVES
315	CALORIES
36.3g	CARBOHYDRATES
8.3g	PROTEIN
13.6g	FAT

INGREDIENTS

- 4 medium carrots, grated
- 1 garlic clove, minced
- ½ tsp ground coriander
- ¼ tsp ground ginger
- ½ tsp cumin seeds
- ½ tsp fennel seeds
- 2 tsp curry powder
- 2tbsp olive oil
- 1 lemon, zest and juice
- Salt and pepper to taste
- 4 pitta breads
- Leafy greens to serve

DIRECTIONS

1. Set your oven to 120C/250F and place your pittas on an oiled baking tray. Place in the oven whilst you make your carrot filling

2. In a large bowl add your carrots and spices, stirring thoroughly to combine. Set aside for 5 minutes to infuse the carrot, and in a separate bowl zest and juice your lemon. Pour in your olive oil and stir. Add this liquid to your spiced carrot, tossing everything together to ensure all the carrot is coated

3. Remove your pittas from the oven and cut in half. Stuff with the carrot mixture, and serve immediately alongside leafy greens

VARIATIONS

Add 4 tbsp of raisins to your carrot mixture for some chewy sweetness, or 4 tbsp of peanuts for a salty crunch!

BARBECUED CAULIFLOWER AND AVOCADO FLATBREADS

Quick and simple, this meal can be whipped up in half an hour. The barbecued cauliflower adds a smokey sweetness that perfectly complements the mashed avocado

4	SERVES
500	CALORIES
65g	CARBOHYDRATES
11g	PROTEIN
25g	FAT

INGREDIENTS

- ½ tsp dark brown sugar
- ½ tsp smoked paprika
- ½ tsp chilli powder
- ½ tsp garlic powder
- ½ tsp ground cumin
- 340g // 1 ½ c cauliflower florets
- 1tbsp olive oil
- 2 avocados
- Salt and pepper to taste
- 4tbsp crushed almonds
- 1tbsp lemon juice

- 4 wholewheat flatbreads / wraps

DIRECTIONS

1. Before starting, preheat your oven to 200C/400F and oil a medium baking tray

2. Place your cauliflower florets on your baking tray before sprinkling over your sugar, spices, and olive oil. Toss everything together before placing in the oven. Roast for 20-25 minutes, or until brown and fragrant

3. Whilst the cauliflower roasts prepare your avocado. Do this by spooning the flesh of both avocados into a bowl and mashing with a fork. Pour in your lemon juice, flavour with salt and pepper, and mix once again

4. To serve divide your avocado and roasted cauliflower between the 4 flatbreads, and top with a sprinkling of crushed almonds

■□■□■□■□■□■□■□

AUBERGINE ARRABBIATA

An Italian classic, spicy tomato sauce with juicy aubergine is a winning mix to take pasta to the next level

4	SERVES
346	CALORIES
57.3g	CARBOHYDRATES
12.8g	PROTEIN
9g	FAT

INGREDIENTS

- 300g // 3c penne pasta, preferably wholewheat
- 500g // 2c aubergines, cut into bite sized chunks
- 1-3 fresh chillies, finely sliced (number of chillies depends on your spice tolerance)
- 4 garlic cloves, minced
- 1 small white onion, sliced
- 1 tin of chopped tomatoes
- 120ml // ½ c water
- 1tbsp olive oil
- Optional fresh basil to serve

■□■□■□■□■□■□■□■□■□

DIRECTIONS

1. Bring a saucepan of salted water to the boil and cook your pasta as per packet instruction. Once cooked to al dente drain and set aside

2. Whilst your pasta cooks place your chopped aubergine into a large bowl. Boil the kettle before pouring the water over the aubergines and leave to soak for 5 minutes. Drain away the water and set aside

3. Heat your olive oil in a large frying pan, and once hot add your onion, chillies, and garlic. Sautee until soft and starting to brown, then add your aubergine and turn the heat to high, stirring regularly to avoid burning

4. Cook the aubergine for 5-7minutes before adding in the tomatoes and water. Lower the heat and leave the sauce to simmer for 10 minutes, or until your aubergines are adequately softened. Add your cooked pasta to the sauce and cook until heated. Garnish with fresh basil and serve immediately

BEANBALLS

Meatballs move over, these bean balls are a delightful vegan alternative. Serve with spaghetti, zoodles, or as they are with spicy tomato sauce

4	SERVES
403	CALORIES
69.9g	CARBOHYDRATES
21.3g	PROTEIN
10.2g	FAT

INGREDIENTS

- 100g // 1c rolled oats
- 500g // 1 ¾ c black bean
- 2 garlic cloves, minced
- 50g // 1c fresh basil, finely chopped
- 1tbsp ground flaxseeds, soaked in 3tbsp lukewarm water
- 8tbsp nutritional yeast
- Tomato sauce (home made or shop bought)

DIRECTIONS

1. Start by placing your oats into a food processor and pulsing until finely ground (to create oat flour). Throw in your black beans, garlic, soaked flaxseed, nutritional yeast, and ¾ of your basil to the food processor and blend until well combined

2. This mix is enough to create 16 meatballs, therefore 5 per serving (you can amend amounts dependent upon your needs). Take 2 tbsp of mix at a time and roll into a ball with your hands. Place all your meatballs on a plate and refrigerate for 20 minutes

3. After chilling cook your meatballs through frying or baking
   TO BAKE
   Preheat your oven to 180C/350F and lightly oil a baking tray. Place your meatballs on the tray and shake it slightly to coat with oil. Place in the centre of the oven for 10-15 minutes, or until golden brown and a little crispy
   TO FRY
   Heat 1tbsp of oil in a large frying pan. Fry on a medium heat, turning regularly, for 5-10 minutes, or until golden brown and a little crispy. If you have to fry in batches add an extra 1tsp of oil per batch

4. To serve, heat your tomato sauce and ladle it over the hot meatballs. Garnish with the set aside basil, and vegan cheese if desired

SWEET POTATO SHEPHERDS PIE

Using sweet potatoes and herbs to give this shepherd's pie an exciting twist, the mushrooms and lentils are a perfect alternative to mince, whilst the marmite adds rich depth

8	SERVES
389	CALORIES
51.3g	CARBOHYDRATES
11.2g	PROTEIN
16.3g	FAT

INGREDIENTS

- 1.2kg sweet potatoes
- 2tbsp vegan butter
- 1 medium white onion, diced
- 2 sticks of celery, sliced
- 2 carrots, peeled and cut unevenly
- 2 garlic gloves, minced
- 25g // 1 c fresh thyme
- 2 tsp mixed herbs
- 150g // 2c button mushrooms, chopped
- 200g // 2 1/3 c chestnut mushrooms, chopped
- 2tbsp balsamic vinegar
- 2tbsp marmite
- 100ml // ½ c vegetable stock
- 2 tins of lentil
- Olive oil
- Salt and pepper to taste

DIRECTIONS

1. Before starting, preheat your oven to 200C/400F, and bring a large saucepan of salted water to the boil. Peel your sweet potatoes and roughly chop into bite sized chunks. Place in the boiling water and reduce to a simmer. Cook for 10-15 minutes, or until tender and mashable

2. When cooked drain the water and set aside. Heat 1tbsp of olive oil in a large frying pan before adding in the onion, celery, carrots, and garlic. Sprinkle over the fresh thyme and fry for 5 minutes. Pour in the mushrooms, balsamic vinegar, and marmite with another 2tbsp of oil, and fry for another 5 minutes. Slowly add the stock to the vegetables and allow to simmer. Once the stock has reduced slightly add the entire contents of your lentil tins

3. Leave the vegetables to simmer on a low heat for 10-15 minutes, and in the meantime make your mash topping. Take the now cooled potatoes and add in the 2tbsp of vegan butter and seasoning. Mash until your desired consistency is reached

4. The vegetable liquid should have thickened to a rich sauce by this stage- transfer them into a large baking or roasting dish. Spread your mash on top and use a fork to create some texture (to help make it crispy). Sprinkle over your mixed herbs before placing in the preheated oven

5. Cook for 20 minutes, or until browned and crisp. If you wish you can remove the pie from the oven and grill it for a few minutes to really crisp up your potatoes. Serve immediately accompanied by roasted veg

VEGAN MACARONI NO-CHEESE

Cashew nuts and nutritional yeast give the creamy, cheesy taste and texture that macaroni cheese is loved for- you'll hardly realise it's entirely cheese free!

8	SERVES
453	CALORIES
61.6g	CARBOHYDRATES
16.6g	PROTEIN
16.9g	FAT

INGREDIENTS

- 1 medium yellow onion, sliced or diced
- 1l soya or nut milk (we recommend cashew milk)
- 150g // 1c cashew nuts
- 2 bay leaves
- 4tbsp vegan butter
- 85g // 2/3 c plain flour
- 2tbsp nutritional yeast
- 1tsp mustard powder
- ½ tsp turmeric powder
- 4 cloves of garlic, minced
- 350g // 3 ½ c dried macaroni

- 4tbsp crushed cashews
- 1 ½ tbsp dried thyme
- Salt and pepper to taste

DIRECTIONS

1. Before starting, preheat your oven to 180C/350F and bring a small saucepan of salted water to the boil. Add your macaroni and cook as per packet instructions, then drain and set aside

2. In a separate saucepan slowly heat your milk to the boil. Add in your cashew nuts and bay leaves, then reduce the heat so the mixture is simmering. Leave like this for 5 minutes before removing from the heat, discarding the bay leaves, and setting aside to cool slightly

3. Once cooled from hot to warm transfer your milk mix to a food processor. Blend on high until the cashews and milk have combined to form a smooth and creamy liquid

4. Heat your oil in a medium, heavy-bottomed pan before adding your sliced onion and minced garlic. Sautee until softened and starting to colour, then transfer to a plate and set aside

5. In the same pan now melt your vegan butter. Spoon in the flour, stirring as you do so to prevent burning and create a paste. Slowly pour the warm blended milk mix into the pan, whisking continuously to create a smooth sauce. Bring to the boil and simmer for 5-10 minutes, or until thickened (it should coat the back of a wooden spoon). Stir in the sautéed onion, yeast, mustard powder, and turmeric powder, then season to taste

6. Add your cooked macaroni to the sauce and stir thoroughly. Transfer to a baking dish (20x30cm) and sprinkle over the crushed cashew and dried thyme

7. Cook the dish in the centre of the oven for 25-30 minutes, or until golden, crispy, and bubbling a little at the edges. Remove from the oven and allow to cool and set slightly before serving

BASIC VEGAN LASAGNE

We've provided the basic vegan lasagne recipe here, so feel free to add extra veg or meat substitutes for a delicious and hearty dinner

8	SERVES
353	CALORIES
46.6g	CARBOHYDRATES
13g	PROTEIN
14.2g	FAT

INGREDIENTS

- 750g // 10c mushrooms, sliced
- 2tbsp marmite
- 3 cans of chopped tomatoes
- 1 medium yellow onion, halved and peeled
- 1l soya or nut milk (we recommend cashew milk)
- 4tbsp vegan butter

- 85g // 2/3 c plain flour
- 2tbsp nutritional yeast
- 1tsp mustard powder
- ½ tsp turmeric powder
- 4 cloves of garlic, minced
- Salt and pepper to taste
- Lasagne sheets
- Vegan cheese, sliced or grated

Optional

- Extra veg to layer, such as spinach, carrots, mushrooms, aubergine, courgette, etc.

DIRECTIONS

1. Before starting, preheat your oven to 220C/430F. Prepare any optional extra veg at this point

2. Start by making your tomato sauce. Place your sliced mushrooms and marmite into a small saucepan over a medium heat. Sautee for 2-3 minutes before covering the pan with a lid for 3-5 minutes. Remove the lid and allow the steam to release before pouring in your tinned tomatoes and seasoning to taste. Leave the sauce to simmer for at least 10 minutes, or until thickened to your liking

3. Heat your oil in a medium, heavy-bottomed pan before adding your sliced onion and minced garlic. Sautee until softened and starting to colour, then transfer to a plate and set aside

4. To make the white sauce slowly heat your milk to the boil in a medium saucepan. Add in one half of your onion and reduce the heat so the mixture is simmering. Leave like this for 5 minutes before removing from the heat, discarding the onion, and leaving to cool slightly

5. In the same pan now melt your vegan butter. Spoon in the flour, stirring as you do so to prevent burning and create a paste. Slowly pour the warm milk into the pan, whisking continuously to create a smooth sauce. Bring to the boil and simmer for 5-10 minutes, or until thickened (it should coat the back of a wooden spoon). Stir in the sautéed onion, yeast, mustard powder, and turmeric powder, then season to taste

6. In a large baking dish start layering your lasagne. Start with a layer of tomato sauce, then lasagne sheets, then white sauce. After the white sauce add in any extra veg you may have prepared, before layering again tomato sauce, lasagne, white sauce etc. Continue layering, repeating this process to create 4 sets, or until your sauces run out. Top your final layer of white sauce with the vegan cheese, and season with salt and pepper

7. Place the lasagne in the preheated oven for 30 minutes, or until golden brown and bubbling- if the lasagne looks like it may be cooking too fast either reduce the oven temperature to 200C/400F, or cover with a layer of tin foil. Once cooked cool slightly, then serve

CREAMY CASHEW GNOCCHI

Fluffy potato gnocchi with a creamy and flavourful sauce- you can't go wrong with that!

4	SERVES
410	CALORIES
63g	CARBOHYDRATES
13.5g	PROTEIN
11g	FAT

INGREDIENTS

- 120g // 4c fresh spinach
- 50g // 1c fresh basil (plus extra to garnish)
- 75g // ½ c cashew nuts, raw
- 3tbsp nutritional yeast
- 1tsp miso paste
- 240ml // 1c cashew milk
- 2 garlic cloves
- 1tsp cornflour
- 500g // 3 ¼ c gnocchi (check its vegan)

DIRECTIONS

1. Start by making your creamy cashew sauce. Place your basil, cashews, yeast, miso, milk, garlic, and cornflour into a food processor. Blend on high to create a smooth sauce. Transfer your sauce to a medium saucepan,

2. Keep your sauce on a low heat whilst you cook your gnocchi- you want your sauce to thicken but be sure to keep an eye on it and stir regularly. Cook your gnocchi as per packet instruction, adding your spinach for the final minute before draining away the water

3. Add your gnocchi and spinach to the thickened sauce and cook for a couple of minutes to ensure everything is combined and heated. Serve immediately and garnish with your extra basil

CHANA MASALA

Naturally vegan, this deeply flavoursome curry can be cooked up in a flash to please any hungry vegans

6	SERVES
169	CALORIES
25.7g	CARBOHYDRATES
7g	PROTEIN
4.6g	FAT

INGREDIENTS

- 2 cans of chickpeas
- 1 can chopped tomatoes
- 1 lime, juice and zest
- 2tsp ground cinnamon
- 1 large white onion, diced
- 3 garlic cloves, minced
- 1 fresh red chilli, finely sliced and deseeded
- 2tbsp freshly grated ginger
- 1tbsp garam masala
- 20g // ½ c fresh coriander, finely chopped
- 1tsp ground cumin
- 1tsp ground turmeric
- 1tbsp Coconut oil
- Salt and pepper to taste

DIRECTIONS

1. In a large saucepan heat your can of chopped tomatoes, the liquid from your chickpeas, the lime zest and juice, and your cinnamon. Leave the sauce to simmer on a low heat

2. Melt your coconut oil in a medium frying pan before adding your onion and garlic. Sautee until the onions have softened and are clear, then add in your chickpeas, chilli, ginger, coriander, and spices. Cook this for 2-3 minutes, or until fragrant, before pouring this spiced chickpea mix into your tomato sauce. Stir thoroughly to combine before leaving to simmer for 15-20 minutes

3. Serve immediately, accompanied by rice, naan bread, or curried cauliflower

10-MINUTE MUSHROOM LINGUINE

Ready in just 10 minutes, this mushroom linguine is a staple to eat homemade on even the busiest of days

6	SERVES
430	CALORIES
62g	CARBOHYDRATES
15g	PROTEIN
15g	FAT

INGREDIENTS

- 1 packet of linguine pasta (500g // 1lb)
- 150g // 2c button mushrooms, chopped
- 200g // 2 ½ c chestnut mushrooms, chopped
- 3tbsp nutritional yeast
- 4 garlic cloves, minced
- 1 small white onion, sliced
- 80ml // 1/3 c olive oil
- Salt and pepper to taste
- Optional vegan parmesan cheese to serve

DIRECTIONS

1. Bring a medium pan of salted water to the boil. Add your pasta and cook as per packet instructions. Drain the pasta but keep 240ml // 1c of the cooking water. Add the nutritional yeast to the water and set aside

2. Whilst your pasta cooks take a large frying pan and heat 1tbsp of oil over a medium-high heat. Add your mushrooms, onion, and garlic, and fry for 5 minutes. Once the mushrooms have browned and softened pour in your remaining oil, pasta, and reserved cooking water. Toss everything together and season generously

3. Serve hot and with an optional sprinkling of vegan parmesan cheese

TOFU KUNG PAO

You don't need to order takeaway- this tofu kung pao is just as good as what you'd get on UberEats!

4	SERVES
282	CALORIES
12.4g	CARBOHYDRATES
17.3g	PROTEIN
18.5g	FAT

INGREDIENTS

- 2tbsp soy sauce
- 4tsp hoisin sauce
- 1tbsp coconut sugar
- 1tbsp rice wine vinegar
- 1/2tsp cornflour
- 450g // 3c firm tofu, cut into 2cm cubes
- 2tbsp sesame oil
- 1 fresh red chilli, deseeded and finely sliced
- 1 garlic clove, minced
- 1tbsp ginger, grated or minced
- 1 red pepper, sliced,
- 3 spring onions, finely sliced
- Crushed peanuts to serve

DIRECTIONS

1. Start by making your sauce- place your soy sauce, hoisin sauce, coconut sugar, vinegar, 1tbsp of sesame oil, and cornflour in a small dish. Mix together thoroughly, then pour over your cubed tofu. Toss everything together to ensure all the tofu is coated, then place in the fridge to marinate for at least 15 minutes

2. Heat your remaining sesame oil in a frying pan or wok. Add your chilli, garlic, and ginger and fry for 1-2 minutes, then add your sliced pepper and spring onions. Fry for a further 2 minutes before transferring to a bowl and setting aside

3. Whilst the pan is still hot pour in your marinated tofu. Fry until the tofu is browned and the marinade has reduced. Be sure to turn your tofu to ensure even frying. Add your fried pepper mix to the tofu and cook for a couple of minutes, making sure everything is coated in the kung pao sauce

4. Serve over rice or noodles, and topped with a sprinkling of crushed peanuts

COURGETTE FRITTERS

The key to courgette fritters is to remove as much liquid from the courgette as you can prior to cooking. These crispy fritters are a delicious light meal or side dish

8	SERVES
142	CALORIES
14.6g	CARBOHYDRATES
2.9g	PROTEIN
7.9g	FAT

INGREDIENTS

- 490g // 3 ½ c grated courgette
- 125g // 1c plain flour
- ½ tbsp baking powder
- 15g // ¼ c nutritional yeast
- 1 garlic clove, minced
- 2 spring onions, finely sliced
- 60g // ¼ c vegan butter, melted
- Salt and pepper to taste
- Olive oil for frying
- Leafy greens and vegan sour cream to serve

DIRECTIONS

1. Start by grating your courgette and placing in a clean dishcloth. Close the dishcloth by spinning the top and squeeze hard to drain any excess moisture, then transfer to kitchen towels and leave for 5-10 minutes to dry further

2. Place the courgette, flour, baking powder, yeast, garlic, and spring onions into a bowl. Mix everything together, then pour in your melted butter and season before mixing once again to form a thick batter- add water a tsp at a time if your batter is too thick

3. Heat 1tbsp of oil in a large frying pan. Ensure the pan is extremely hot before spooning in your batter, 1/8 at a time- you will probably have to cook in 2 batches, so after the first 4 add another 1tsp of oil

4. Press your batter down to form a rough circle and fry for 2-4 minutes, or until browned and crispy, before flipping. Repeat for the other side

5. Serve warm with a dollop of vegan sour cream and leafy greens

DESSERTS

AVOCADO, PINEAPPLE, AND STRAWBERRY ICE CREAM

Sweet, tart, creamy and refreshing- if you want it in a hurry freeze your fruit beforehand and simply blend!

4	SERVES
94	CALORIES
4g	CARBOHYDRATES
3g	PROTEIN
7g	FAT

INGREDIENTS

- 100g // 2/3 c strawberries, chopped
- 100g // ½ c pineapples, cubed
- 1 avocado
- 1tsp coconut sugar
- 2tbsp fresh mint, roughly sliced
- Dried pineapple to top

DIRECTIONS

1. Stone your avocado and spoon out the flesh. Place all ingredients except the dried pineapple into a food processor and blend until smooth, then transfer to a container and place in the freezer. Freeze for at least 5 hours, but be sure to stir every hour or so to ensure the ice cream doesn't freeze solid, and maintains a creamy texture

2. An hour or so before serving mix for a final time and place dried pineapple and any extra mint on the top to decorate. Serve accompanied by fresh strawberries and pineapple if desired

CHOCOLATE BROWNIES

These rich and fudgy brownies can compete with any non-vegan recipe easily. Top with coconut cream and cherries for a decadent dessert

12	SERVES
269	CALORIES
36g	CARBOHYDRATES
4g	PROTEIN
15g	FAT

INGREDIENTS

- 2tbsp ground flaxseed, soaked in 6tbsp of water for at least 5 minutes
- 80g // 1/3 c vegan butter
- 1tsp instant coffee granules
- 120g // ¾ c vegan dark chocolate chips
- 4tbsp water
- 125g // 1c self-raising flour
- ¼ tsp baking powder
- 50g // ½ c cocoa powder
- 1/2tsp salt
- 70g // 2/3 c ground almonds

- 250g // 1 ¼ c golden caster sugar
- ½ tbsp vanilla extract

DIRECTIONS

1. Before cooking preheat your oven to 170/330F, and line a 20x20cm baking tin with parchment paper

2. Place butter, coffee granules, water, and chocolate chips in a large mixing bowl over a bain marie and melt over a low heat. Remove from the heat and set aside to cool slightly

3. Using a handheld whisk, beat your sugar into your cooled chocolate mixture until the sugar is dissolved and the mix is smooth and glossy. Stir in the vanilla and soaked flaxseed

4. Sift flour, baking powder, cocoa powder, and salt into the chocolate mix, then pour in the ground almonds and fold everything together- the batter will be very thick

5. Transfer the brownie batter to your lined baking tin and bake in the centre of the oven. After 30 minutes insert a skewer to check on the cooking, and dependent upon your preference for gooiness leave for a further 5-10 minutes

6. Remove from the oven and allow to cool for 15-20 minutes before cutting into squares and serving

BANANA CREAM PIE

Bursting with flavour, this pie is always a crowd pleaser- be sure to grab a slice because it'll be gone in minutes!

8	SERVES
369	CALORIES
33.7g	CARBOHYDRATES
5g	PROTEIN
25.9g	FAT

INGREDIENTS

Filling

- 1 medium banana, mashed
- 360ml // 1 ½ c nut milk

Coconut Whipped Cream

- 1 can coconut cream, refrigerated overnight

Base

- 90g // 1 c rolled oats
- 60g // ½ c almonds
- 60 ml // ¼ c melted coconut oil
- 2tbsp cane or coconut sugar
- 1 banana sliced

- 70g // 1/3 c cane or coconut sugar
- 1 tsp vanilla extract

- 1/2tsp vanilla extract
- 3tbsp icing sugar

DIRECTIONS

1. Before starting, preheat your over to 180C/350F, and line a 8x8 baking tin with parchment paper

2. Start by placing all your 'filling' ingredients in a small pan. Whisk until thoroughly blended, then transfer to the stove and heat on medium-high, whisking continuously, until it starts to bubble. Once bubbling turn the heat to low and cook until thickened. Transfer to a bowl and allow to cool before covering with clingfilm and placing in the fridge for at least 2 hours

3. Remove your coconut cream from the fridge and gently open. Scoop into a chilled bowl the firm cream (leave the watery part) and beat with a handheld whisk. Add the vanilla extract and icing sugar, then beat again before placing in the fridge to chill

4. Whilst the cream fillings cool prepare your base. To do this, add your oats and almonds to a food processor and blend until it forms a fine, floury texture. Add your melted coconut oil and sugar, and blend once again until a loose dough forms- add an extra 1tsp of coconut oil if the mixture is too dry and crumbly to hold some shape

5. Pour your base mix into the prepared baking tin and flatten. Place into the preheated oven and bake for 15-20 minutes, or until the edges are golden and the centre is starting to brown. Remove from the oven and set aside to cool

6. To assemble arrange your sliced banana on the cooked base. Pour over the thickened and cooled filling and smooth before then pouring over the coconut whipped cream. Swirl the coconut cream into the banana filling

7. Cover with clingfilm and refrigerate for a further 4 hours (ideally overnight) before cutting into 8 slices and serving

NO BAKE COCONUT CHEESECAKE BARS

Our no bake cheesecake bars are a fantastically easy way to impress anyone!
Creamy coconut on a chewy sweet base- could it be any better?

10	SERVES
360	CALORIES
44g	CARBOHYDRATES
7g	PROTEIN
21g	FAT

INGREDIENTS

Base

- 175g // 1 ¼ c almonds, raw
- 220g // 1 ¼ c dates, pitted

Filling

- 210g // 1 ½ c cashew nuts, raw
- 150g // ¾ c coconut sugar
- 1 can of coconut cream (380g // 13.5oz.)
- 60ml // ¼ c melted coconut oil
- 1 lemon, zest and juice
- Dried coconut flakes to top
- Strawberries to garnish

- ½ tsp salt

DIRECTIONS

1. Before starting line a 11x7 baking tin with parchment. Bring a saucepan of water to the boil, add your cashew nuts and simmer for 20-25 minutes, or until softened. Drain and set aside

2. Place your almonds, dates, and salt into a food processor and blend until a smooth and sticky mixture forms. Pour into your lined tin and press down firmly to create an even base

3. Place your soaked cashews, coconut cream, sugar, coconut oil, lemon juice and zest into a food processor and blend until a smooth and creamy mix forms. Pour this over your base and top with dried coconut flakesTransfer the layered mix to the freezer to set- roughly 5 hours. Once set and firm to the touch remove from the freezer and thaw for a few minutes before cutting into 10 portions

4. Serve garnished with fresh strawberries

RED VELVET FUDGE BITES

A bite of heaven... with hidden vegetables! Keep these in the fridge for a quick morsel of velvety joy

18	SERVES
120	CALORIES
4g	CARBOHYDRATES
4g	PROTEIN
10.5g	FAT

INGREDIENTS

- 170g // 1c raw cashew nuts
- 125g // 1/2 c beetroot puree
- 180ml // 2/3 c cashew milk
- 1 vanilla bean pod
- 1tsp liquid sweetener (eg stevia or erythritol)
- 1tbsp vanilla extract
- 110g // 1/2c cacao butter, melted
- 50g // 2 scoops chocolate protein powder
- 2tbsp cocoa powder

DIRECTIONS

1. Before cooking place the cashew nuts, beetroot puree, and cashew milk in a bowl. Stir everything together before adding in the whole vanilla bean pod and then covering with clingfilm. Place in the fridge to infuse for at least 6 hours

2. Once infused, line an 8x8 baking tin with parchment paper, and take your cashew mix from the fridge. Remove the whole vanilla bean pod before pouring the mix into a food processor and blending until completely smooth

3. Add the liquid sweetener, vanilla extract, and melted cacao butter, then blend again. Finally, add your vanilla protein powder and cocoa powder. Blend until the mix is combined, thick, and creamy, then pour into your prepared tin

4. Spread and smooth the mixture, then place in the fridge to set. Leave the fudge for at least 12 hours (ideally overnight) before removing from the fridge. This recipe is designed to produce 18 fudge bites, so cut 6 by 3 before transferring to a plate and serving

APPLE AND PLUM CRUMBLE

Reminiscent of childhood, this crumble is sweet and spicy, packed with delicious stewed fruit for a comforting pudding any day of the week

12	SERVES
279	CALORIES
42.9g	CARBOHYDRATES
2.8g	PROTEIN
11.3g	FAT

INGREDIENTS

Stewed fruit

- 4 large cooking apples
- 4 plums
- ½ lemon, zest and juice
- 60ml // ¼ c water
- ½ c sugar

- 1tsp fresh ginger, grated
- 2 tsp ground cinnamon
- ½ tsp nutmeg
- 1/2tsp ginger
- Pinch of salt

Crumble

- 100g // 1c rolled oats
- 70g // 3/4c almond flour
- 150g // ¾ c brown sugar
- 50g // ½ cup almonds, chopped
- 1tbsp vanilla extract

- 8tbsp coconut oil, softened but not melted
- Pinch of salt

DIRECTIONS

1. Before starting, preheat your oven to 180C/350F. Peel your apples and roughly chop into bite sized pieces, then destone and roughly chop your plums

2. Place all the 'stewed fruit' ingredients in a saucepan and stir thoroughly to combine. Place over a low heat, covering the pan with a lid but leaving space for steam to escape. Heat for 10-15 minutes, or until the apples have softened slightly, being sure to stir every few minutes to ensure even cooking. Once slightly softened pour the mix into a large baking dish and spread evenly

3. Make your crumble by first mixing the oats, flour, almonds, and sugar in a medium bowl. Add in your vanilla extract, and your coconut oil 1tbsp at a time. Mix with your hands or a fork to create a lumpy, crumbly texture. Spread this evenly on top of your apples

4. Place the dish into the centre of the oven and cook for 40-45 minutes, or until the top is golden brown and crispy, and you can see some of the apple mixture bubbling at the sides. Remove from the oven and serve warm

CHOCOLATE AND PEANUT RAW COOKIE DOUGH BOWLS

The classic combo of chocolate and peanut... in a perfectly edible cookie dough!
An indulgent dessert everyone will want more of

6	SERVES
286	CALORIES
32g	CARBOHYDRATES
7g	PROTEIN
15g	FAT

INGREDIENTS

- 1 can of chickpeas, drained, rinsed, and dried

- 2tsp vanilla extract

- 4tbsp maple syrup

- 2tbsp cocoa powder

- 120g // ½ c peanut butter

- ¼ tsp salt

- 45g // ¼ c dark chocolate chips

- 30g // ¼ c peanuts, chopped

- Optional peanut butter and banana to serve

DIRECTIONS

1. Place your chickpeas, vanilla extract, maple syrup, cocoa powder, peanut butter, and salt into a food processor. Blend on high until combined, smooth, and creamy

2. Transfer the dough mix to a bowl. Sprinkle over your chocolate chips and peanuts, then fold into to the dough, mixing thoroughly to ensure the chocolate and peanuts run evenly throughout the dough, then spoon into serving bowls

3. Serve topped with an optional drizzle of peanut butter and sliced banana

VANILLA PUDDING POTS

Classic vanilla, the silken tofu used in these puddings boosts the protein and creates a smooth creamy texture with every mouthful

4	SERVES
248	CALORIES
44g	CARBOHYDRATES
10g	PROTEIN
6g	FAT

INGREDIENTS

- 900g // 5 c silken tofu
- 120ml // ½ c maple syrup
- Pinch of salt
- 1 whole vanilla bean pod
- 3 tbsp arrowroot powder or cornflour
- 280ml // 2/3 + 1/2 c almond milk
- Optional berries to top

DIRECTIONS

1. Place your tofu, maple syrup, salt, and 160ml//2/3c almond milk into a food processor. Blend on high until smooth, then transfer to a small saucepan, add your vanilla bean pod and heat to simmering

2. In a separate bowl whisk together your remaining milk and arrowroot powder. Pour this into the simmering tofu mix and whisk to combine

3. Continue whisking for a couple of minutes, or until the mixture is starting to thicken. Do not let the mixture thicken too much- remove from the heat whilst still pourable

4. Remove your vanilla bean pod and divide the mixture evenly between 4 pots. Cover each with clingfilm and place in the fridge to set. Leave for at least 3 hours, but preferably overnight. Once set remove from the fridge. Top with optional seasonal berries and serve

BERRY MOUSSE

Using aquafaba as an alternative to egg whites, throw in any seasonal berries for this light and summery pudding you won't even realise is vegan!

4	SERVES
143	CALORIES
16.1g	CARBOHYDRATES
1.3g	PROTEIN
9.1g	FAT

INGREDIENTS

- 150g // 2/3 c coconut cream
- ¾ tsp agar powder, dissolved in 1tbsp water
- 200g // 2c fresh seasonal berries
- 1tsp vanilla extract
- 60ml // ¼ c maple syrup
- 85g // 1/3 c aquafaba (this is the liquid you will find in canned chickpeas)
- 1/8tsp cream of tartar

DIRECTIONS

1. Place your coconut cream and dissolved agar into a medium saucepan-whisk continuously over a medium heat until it starts to boil, then remove from the heat to cool slightly

2. Place your berries, vanilla extract, and maple syrup in a food processor and blend on high until a thin juice forms. Pour the juice into your cooled coconut mix and stir to combine

3. Pour your aquafaba into a large bowl and sprinkle over your cream of tartar. Using a handheld whisk, whip the mixture of the highest speed until stiff peaks form

4. Slowly pour half of the berry mixture into your whipped aquafaba. Use a spatula to gently fold the berry mix in, making sure to keep as much air as possible. Once combined add the remaining half of the berry mix, and repeat the gentle folding process

5. Divide the mixture between 4 jars and cover each with clingfilm. Place in the fridge for at least 3 hours to set, but preferably overnight. Serve topped with fresh seasonal berries

ORANGE AND CRANBERRY LOAF CAKE

The classic flavours of cranberry and orange combine to create a sweet and fruity loaf cake that's perfect for afternoon tea

10	SERVES
149	CALORIES
34.5g	CARBOHYDRATES
3.4g	PROTEIN
0.7g	FAT

INGREDIENTS

- 280g // 2c plain flour
- 2tsp baking powder
- ½ tsp bicarbonate of soda
- ½ tsp ground ginger
- 150g // 2/3 c golden caster sugar
- 240ml // 1 c fresh orange juice
- Zest of 1 orange
- 115g // ½ c applesauce, unsweetened
- 130g // 1 heaped c cranberries, fresh or frozen
- Sprinkling of dried cranberries

DIRECTIONS

1. Before starting, preheat your oven to 180C/350F, and line a standard loaf tin with parchment paper

2. Sift flour, baking powder, bicarbonate of soda, and ginger together into a medium mixing bowl. Add your caster sugar and stir everything to combine before pouring your orange juice and applesauce over the dry mix. Stir everything together until the flour is just combined

3. Sprinkle over your orange zest and cranberries, and stir once again until they are equally distributed throughout the batter, then pour into the prepared loaf tin and sprinkle over a few dried cranberries. Bake in the centre of the oven for 45-50 minutes. Check it is cooked by inserting a skewer- if cooked the skewer will be dry upon removal

Leave to cool slightly before slicing. Serve with optional fresh berries and coconut

Printed in Great Britain
by Amazon